LEARN SCIENCE WITH MO

ENERGY

Paul Mason

Michael Buxton

Enslow PUBLISHING

Published in 2026 by Enslow Publishing, LLC
2544 Clinton Street
Buffalo, NY 14224

First published in Great Britain in 2023 by Wayland

Editor: John Hort
Design: Collaborate
Illustrations: Michael Buxton

Manufactured in the United States of America

CPSIA compliance information: Batch #CSENS26: For further information contact Enslow Publishing LLC, New York, New York at 1-800-398-2504.

Please visit our website, www.enslowpublishing.com. For a free color catalog of all our high-quality books, call toll free 1-800-398-2504 or fax 1-877-980-4454.

Cataloging-in-Publication Data
Names: Mason, Paul. | Buxton, Michael, illustrator.
Title: Energy / Paul Mason ; illustrated by Michael Buxton.
Description: Buffalo, NY : Enslow Publishing, 2026. | Series: Learn science with Mo | Includes glossary and index.
Identifiers: ISBN 9781978544666 (pbk.) | ISBN 9781978544673 (library bound) | ISBN 9781978544680 (ebook)
Subjects: LCSH: Force and energy--Juvenile literature. | Power resources--Juvenile literature.
Classification: LCC TJ163.23 M376 2026 | DDC 621.042--dc23

Find us on

SAFETY PRECAUTIONS

We recommend adult supervision at all times while making the recipes in this book.
Some of the equipment needed to make the recipes in this book can be dangerous if not handled correctly.
Please follow the instructions carefully and always ask an adult to help when the instructions tell you to.

Children should always be supervised when working with hot materials or knives. Some ingredients may contain nuts, seeds, eggs, yeast, or other allergens. Always check the packaging for any allergens that may cause an allergic reaction. Anyone with a known allergy must avoid these.

Contents

The words in **bold** are in the glossary on page 30.

ENERGY FOR MO

Mo and Sid have been swimming. Now they are tired and want to eat. They need to eat to get more energy.

Without energy it would not be possible for our bodies to work. Mo, what activities do you use energy for?

SWIMMING! AND RUNNING ... SKATEBOARDING ... UM ...

How about thinking? Your brain actually uses more energy than any muscle.

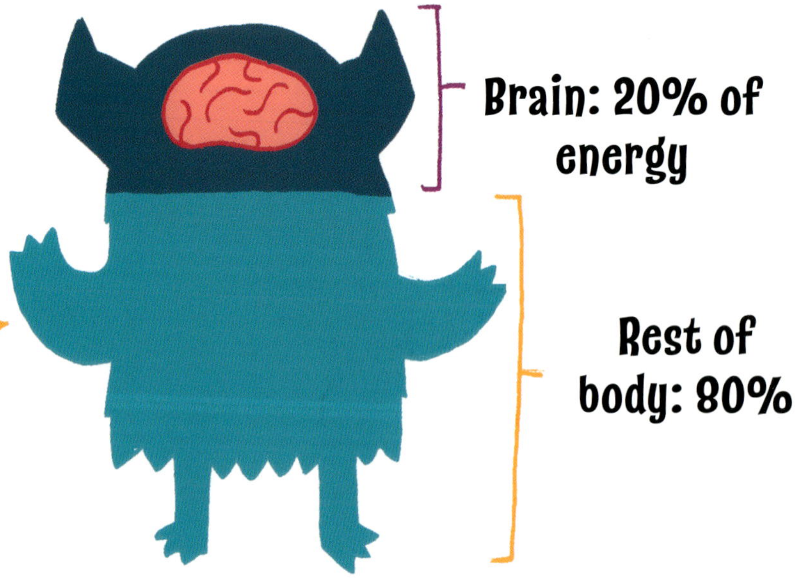

THINKING DOES MAKE ME TIRED ...

Like monsters, all living things need energy to stay alive. They get this energy from food.

I LIKE FOOD!
I CAN'T REALLY COOK, THOUGH ...

Mo, that is no problem. Later, you and Cousin Rory are taking a cooking class. You are going to learn about cooking ... and baking cakes.

WOO!

We're off to make cakes!

The class is not only going to teach you about cooking. You are also going to learn more about energy.

Energy is what makes our world work. It lets us do everything from breathing to thinking or kicking a ball. Energy heats and cools our homes. Energy powers our cars and buses. It is used to **manufacture** lots of things we use. It also helps us cook.

WARMTH FROM THE SUN

Before Mo starts cooking, he needs to dry off with Sid. Their swim made them cold. Mo warms up after he eats, but Sid does not. This is because Sid is a snake, a cold-blooded animal.

Cold-blooded
Body cannot keep itself warm

Warm-blooded
Body keeps itself warm

Cold-blooded animals like Sid do not use energy from food to keep themselves warm. They need to get heat from somewhere else instead.

HOW CAN SID WARM UP, THEN?

Lying in the sunshine for awhile will warm Sid up. The sun's light contains a lot of energy. It can be very hot.

Stops skin from being burned by the sun's energy

Mo, which of these other living things need the sun's energy to stay alive? (Warning: this is a trick question!) The answers are on page 32.

PLANT-POWERED ENERGY

A lot of our energy comes from the sun. Before we can use it, though, this energy is usually stored somewhere else. Often it is stored in plants.

Plants grow by using energy from the sun, plus water, and a **gas** called carbon dioxide to make their own food.

How plants make food

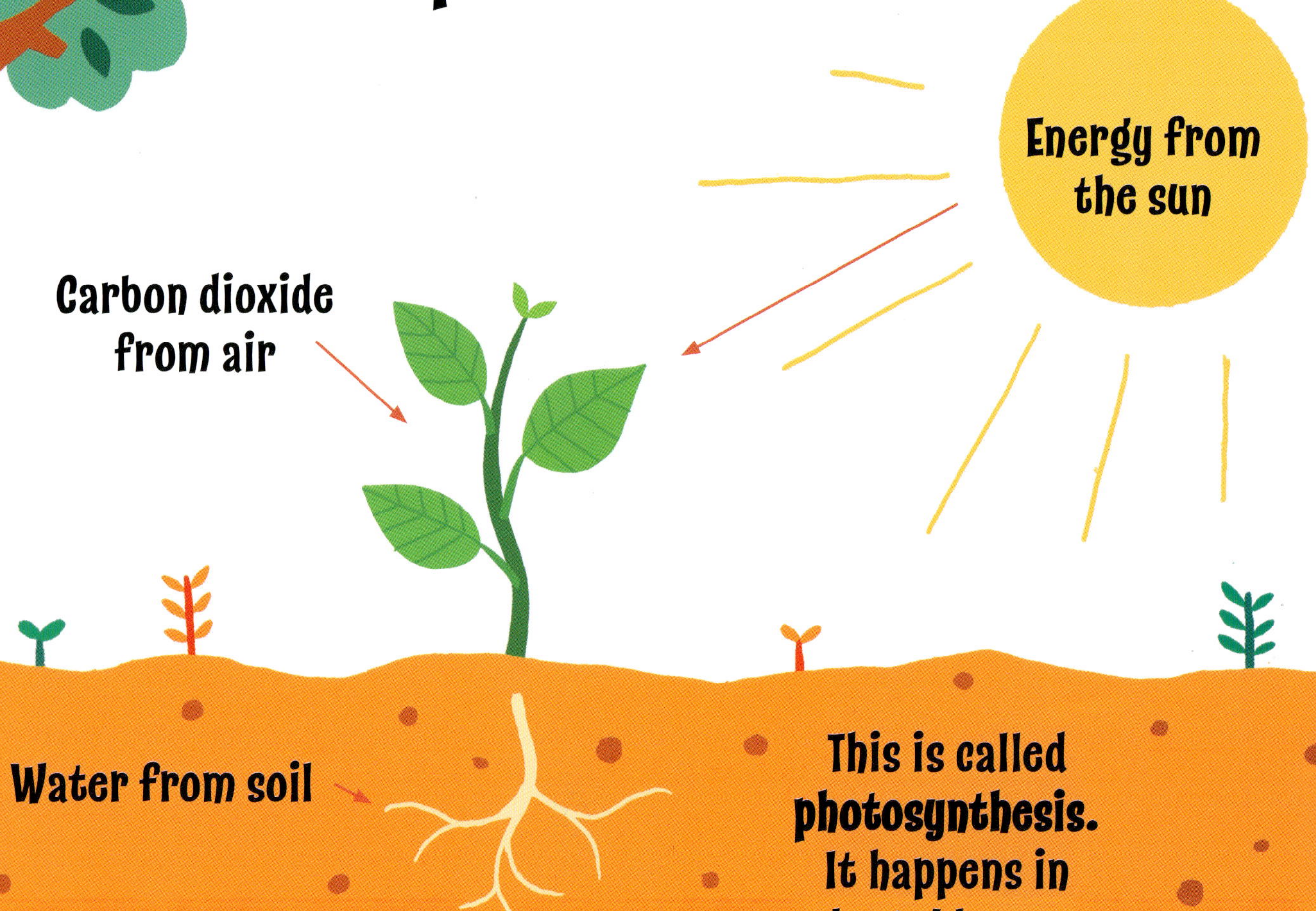

This is called photosynthesis. It happens in plants' leaves.

As they grow, plants store energy from the sun in their roots, stem, branches, and leaves. This stored energy can be released in different ways.

When you eat part of a plant, some of the energy it has stored passes into your body.

Gasoline (and other **fossil fuels**) is made of tiny plants and animals that died millions of years ago (see page 13).

Movement energy can be released when they are burned.

Setting wood on fire releases some of the tree's stored energy as heat and light.

Even the energy in meat came originally from plants. The energy in a beef burger came from a cow that ate plants.

Grass stores sun's energy

Cow stores energy from grass

Beef burger

RENEWABLE ENERGY

So, Mo, you have learned how the sun gives us a store of energy by helping plants to grow. Can you think of other ways the sun gives us energy?

TOTALLY! SOLAR PANELS MAKE ELECTRICITY.

Great answer! You are correct: We do use **solar panels** to make electricity. Here's how ...

1) Sunlight hits solar panel

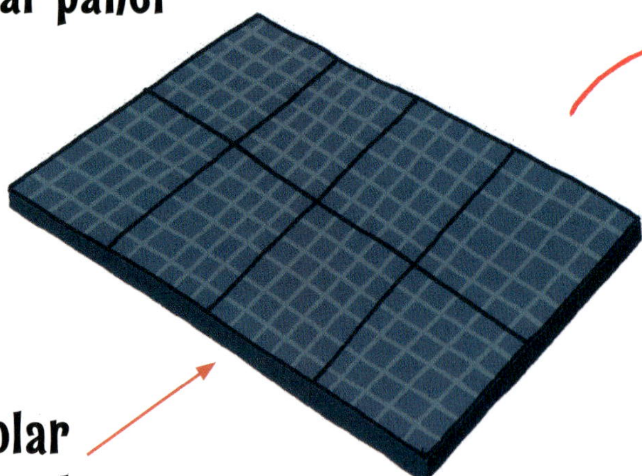

Solar panel

2) Electricity flows from solar panel to homes

3) Electricity provides energy

Energy that will not run out, such as energy from the sun*, is called **renewable** energy.

*This will not run out until the sun dies out (in about 4.5 billion years).

Can you think of other kinds of renewable energy, Mo?

Those are great answers! We sometimes use energy from all those things:

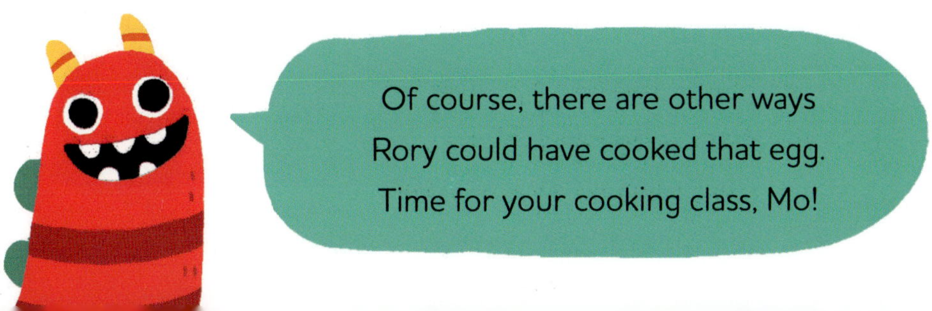

GAS-POWERED EGGS

When Mo and Rory arrive at their cooking class, they find out the first lesson is about breakfast. They are going to make scrambled eggs on toast.

We've had breakfast ...

BUT WE COULD EAT ANOTHER!

First they break the eggs into a bowl. Then the eggs have to be **whisked**. Whisking is hard work! Where does the energy you're using come from, Mo?

THE FOOD I HAD FOR MY FIRST BREAKFAST!

Correct, Mo! Now, to cook the eggs we need heat energy. The teacher turns on the gas flame underneath the pan. Where does the gas come from, Mo?

MILLIONS OF YEARS AGO!

Good answer: You remembered what was on page 9. Well done. But the question was "where," not "when" ...

The story began when tiny plants and animals died and sank to the bottom of the sea.

Millions of years later, their remains had formed natural gas trapped between layers of rock. People removed it (as well as oil).

Today this gas can be used in the cooking class...

... and start a fire under your pan.

ELECTRIC TOAST

While Mo cooks the eggs, Rory is in charge of toast. The bread goes into the toaster and Rory sets the timer for three minutes.

Investigating how the bread gets toasted shows us one of the cooking processes that energy makes possible.

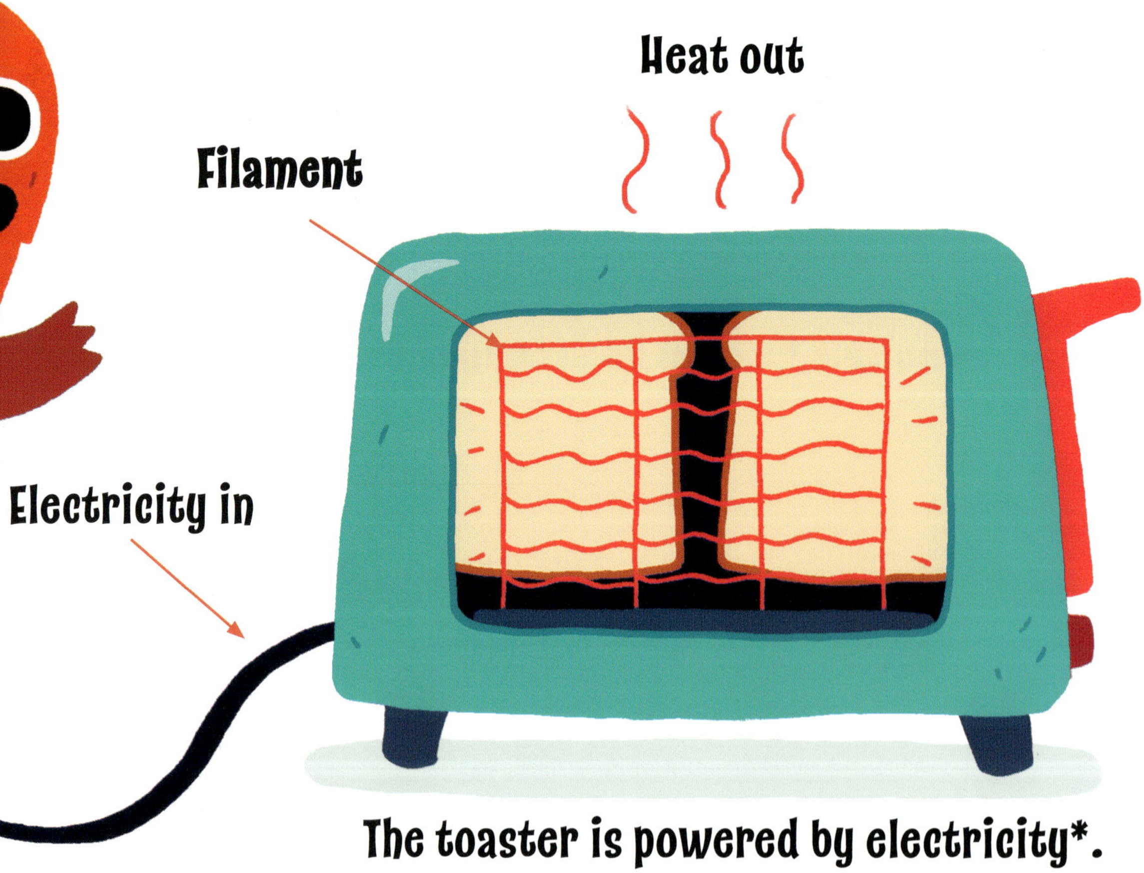

The toaster is powered by electricity*.

*Electricity is made in lots of different ways. See page 28 to find out more.

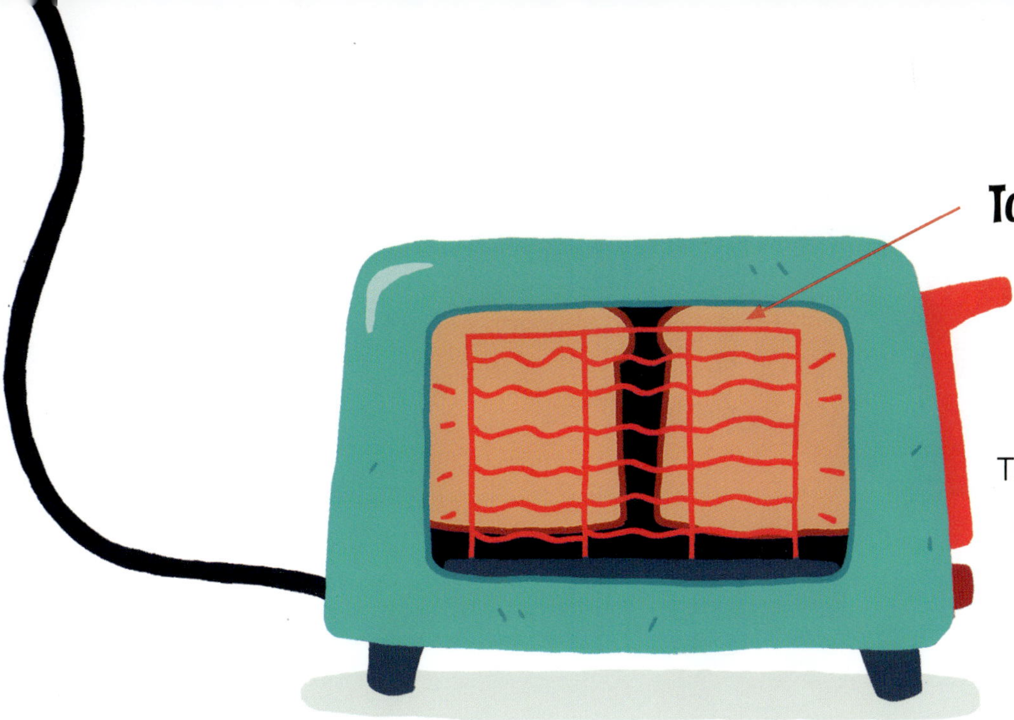

The electricity flows into the toaster and heats metal filaments.

The energy from the glow of the filaments passes to the bread and turns it into toast.

The bread gets browner and browner until ...

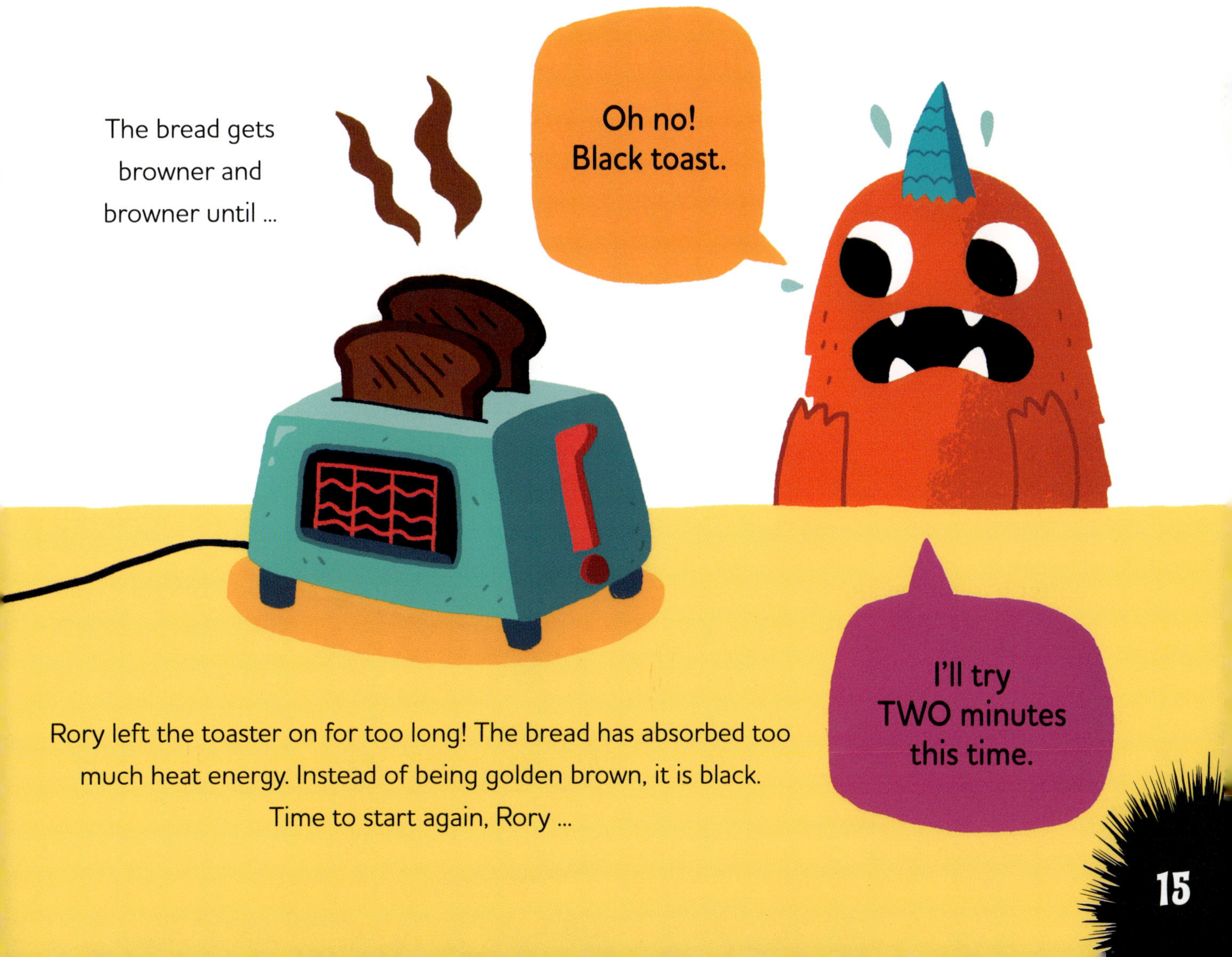

Rory left the toaster on for too long! The bread has absorbed too much heat energy. Instead of being golden brown, it is black. Time to start again, Rory ...

HOT ENOUGH TO MELT BUTTER

Just as the eggs are cooked, the toast pops up. Rory butters it, ready for the eggs to go on top.

Mo turns around, looks at the toast and starts to put on MORE butter.

Stop, Mo! It has already been buttered.

The butter has **melted** into the hot toast. It did this because heat energy turned the butter from hard, to soft, and then **liquid**. Heat energy melted the butter, like this ...

Stage 1: toast, layer of **solid**, unmelted butter on top.

Can you and Rory think of any other objects that heat energy changes in this way, Mo?

Do you agree with Mo? Turn to page 32 to find out if you are right.

Finally breakfast is ready and it's only 11 o'clock! After all that work, no wonder you and Rory are hungry again, Mo.

Stage 2: half the layer of butter has melted into the toast.

Stage 3: solid butter has completely melted into liquid butter.

PROJECT BROWNIE

Mo and Rory, it is time for the most important part of your class. You are going to learn how to make your favorite snack: chocolate brownies.

The first job is melting butter and chocolate chunks.

If they get hot too quickly, butter and chocolate do not mix properly. The ingredients have to be heated up very gently. You are going to learn a cooking technique designed to LOSE heat energy at each stage.

1. Boil some water, then turn it down to a **simmer**.

2. Next put an empty, heat safe bowl into the pan. (It can touch the water, but not the bottom of the pan.)

3. Add the chocolate and butter to the bowl. Then melt them slowly.

So much heat energy is escaping from the sides of the pan and in the form of steam that only a little goes into the butter and chocolate. They melt nice and slowly.

4. The chocolate and butter melt together to make a lovely smooth liquid.

Even though the mixture has been cooked gently, it is still too hot to taste.

ELECTRIC VS MUSCLE ENERGY

Stage two of making brownies is to put **egg whites** and sugar into two bowls. Then Mo and Rory add air to the mixture to make it fluffy. They do this with hand whisks.

After all that work whisking the eggs, Mo grabs a battery-powered electric whisk.

The electric whisk uses electrical energy to create movement.

Rory's old-fashioned hand whisk uses his energy to create movement.

How many other things can you think of that use batteries, Mo?

Batteries are a way to store energy. Batteries release electricity in a kind of tug-of-war between two bits of different types of metal. One bit is called "positive" and the other "negative."

Unless the battery is connected, these two don't work together:

But when the battery is connected ...

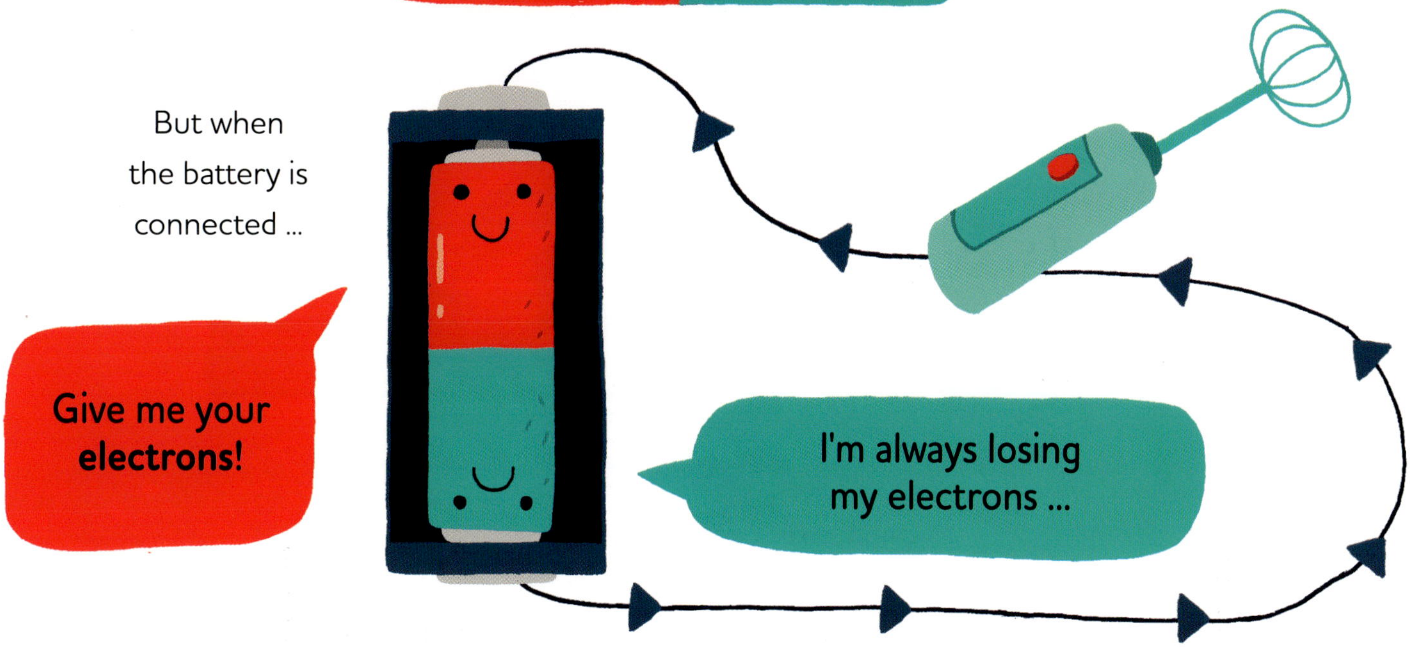

Electrons flow from negative to positive. This creates an electrical current, which can give energy to (among other things) a whisk.

THE RIGHT TEMPERATURE

Mo puts their chocolatey mixture in with the whisked-egg mixture. Rory sifts some flour and cocoa powder into a bowl.

Mo mixes in the flour and cocoa powder. It all goes into a brownie tray, and is cooked at 350°F (180°C).

The oven uses electrical energy.

The electrical energy heats metal.

The hot metal releases heat and warms up the inside of the oven.

When it reaches 350°F, the brownies are put into the oven.

Baking brownies

Temperature measures how much heat energy an object has. It is usually measured in degrees Celsius (°C) or degrees Fahrenheit (°F).

The hot air will heat the baking tray and brownie mixture.

Too hot to eat

VOLCANOES! AND ... ICE.

Good answers! The **lava** in volcanoes has a temperature of about 1,832°F (1,000°C). Ice has a temperature of 32°F (0°C).

DING DONG!

Mo's friends Sid, Dizzy, and Dozy have come to try the brownies ... but no one knows they are outside! The doorbell is not working.

Finally, Dizzy starts banging on the door. The teacher comes to let them in and says she will fix the doorbell, in case anyone else arrives.

Battery-powered doorbell

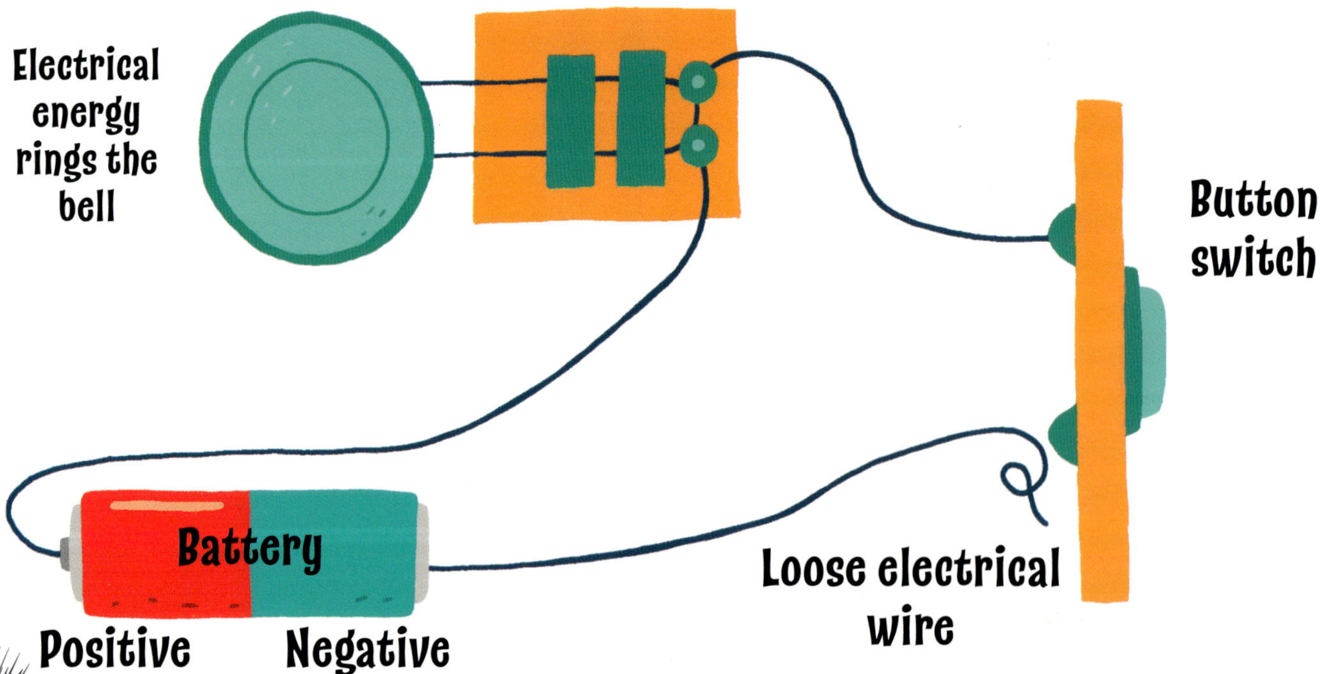

Pressing the doorbell should make a loop (or circuit) for electricity to flow along as long as everything is working.

First, the teacher changes the battery, in case the store of energy in the old one ran out.

The issue is not the battery. Next she looks at the connections between different parts of the loop. Under the bell cover, one has come loose!

Loose wire means electricity cannot flow

With the wire in place, electricity flows

BECAUSE THAT'S WHEN ELECTRICITY HAS A LOOP TO FLOW AROUND?

Correct! And why did the doorbell not ring for Sid, Dozy, and Dizzy?

BECAUSE EVEN WHEN THEY PRESSED THE BUTTON, THE ELECTRICITY STILL DIDN'T HAVE A LOOP TO FLOW AROUND.

Also correct!

LIGHTS OUT

Mo and Rory's brownies have cooled down enough to eat. Mo, what would the scientific description for "cooled down" be?

I KNOW THIS!
"LOST HEAT ENERGY."

Excellent answer, you are correct. Your friends are here to try the brownies and so are some special judges. Except ...

CLICK!

The lights!

That was a good suggestion, but the lights are not battery- powered. The teacher turns on her flashlight and discovers what really happened ...

Turn those back on!

Sid turned off the lights at the **crucial** moment, for a joke! Everyone is annoyed, so Sid turns them back on ...

CLICK!

One ...

CLICK!

two ...

CLICK!

three ...

CLICK!

four.

And the room is lit up again. Totally correct, well done!

BECAUSE EVERY TIME A SWITCH TURNS ON, ELECTRICAL ENERGY GOES TO ANOTHER LIGHT.

QUICK QUIZ

1 What is the name for the loop that electricity flows around?

a) a hoop

b) a roundabout

c) a circuit.

2 What could stop electricity from flowing?

a) a broken wire

b) a battery running out

c) turning off a switch

d) all of those.

Find out if you were right on page 32.

WHERE ELECTRICITY COMES FROM

Buildings usually get electricity from a big cable that comes in from outside. The system that brings it is called a grid. But where does the grid get its energy?

That's right, Mo. Most power stations use machines called turbines to make electricity.

Turning turbines

1) A propellor-like device called a rotor spins.

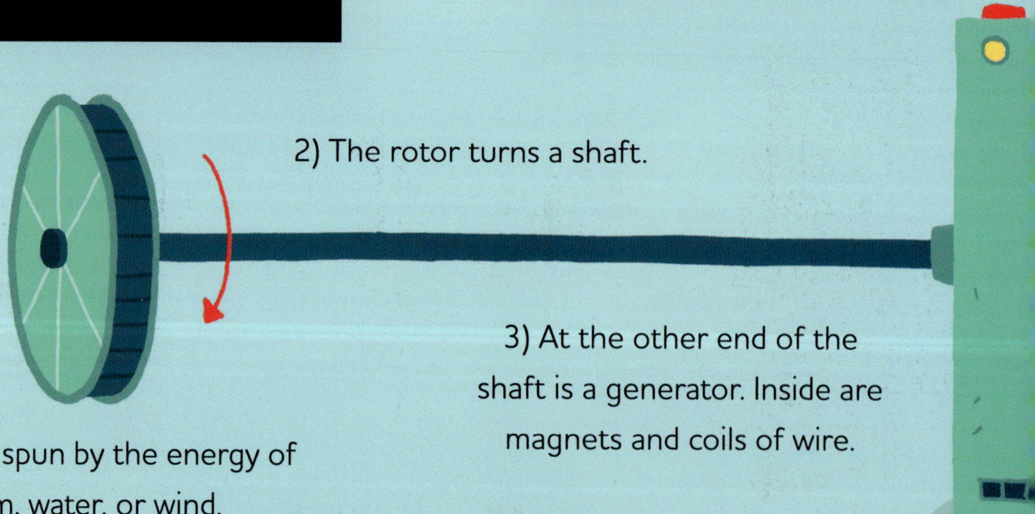

2) The rotor turns a shaft.

3) At the other end of the shaft is a generator. Inside are magnets and coils of wire.

Usually rotors are spun by the energy of flowing steam, water, or wind.

Over half of the world's electricity is made by burning **coal** or gas. This releases heat energy. The heat energy is used to make steam.

The steam is forced through a narrow space—like the spout of the boiling teapot behind you, Mo. The steam spins rotors and the rotors turn an electrical generator. However, coal and gas release pollution, which harms the planet.

Renewable energy, made by solar panels or wind turbines for example, is much healthier for the planet.

In 1831, an inventor called Michael Faraday discovered that spinning magnets inside coils of wire produces electricity. This is how generators work.

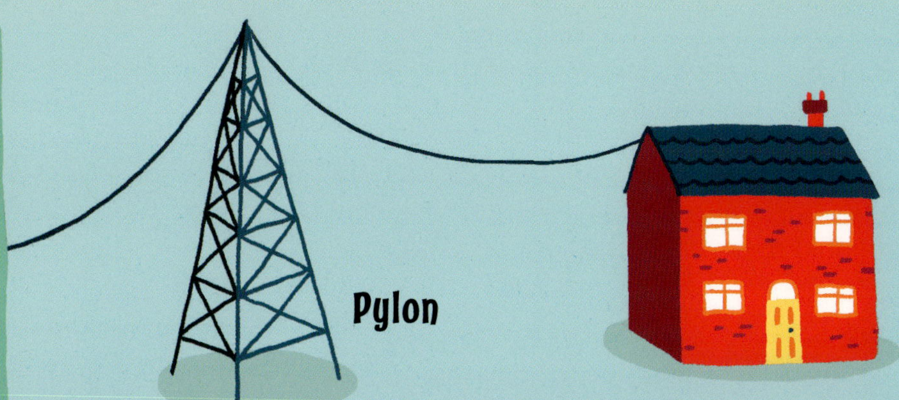

4) Electricity from the generator is fed into the grid ...

5) ... then to homes and other places through power lines.

Glossary

coal
hard, black or brown material found mainly underground

crucial
so important that without it, an event cannot happen

egg white
clear, gloopy liquid inside an egg that is not the yolk (the yellow part in the middle)

electron
one of the three main parts of an atom (a tiny piece of an element)

filament
long, thin wire

fossil fuel
fuel made of plants and/or animals that died millions of years ago. Fossil fuels, such as coal, oil, and natural gas, are usually found underground.

gas
something that will spread out to fill whatever space is available to it

lava
hot liquid rock that comes out of a volcano

liquid
material that changes shape to fit whatever container it is inside, but is always the same volume

manufacture
to make goods, often in a factory

melt
turn from solid (for example, ice) to liquid (for example, water)

photosynthesis
how plants make their own food, using sunlight, carbon dioxide, and water

renewable
when talking about energy, renewable means something that will not run out

simmer
boil very gently

solar panel
solar cells in a solar panel capture the sun's energy, causing electrons to move and create an electric current

solid
material that stays the same size and shape

SPF
short for Sun Protection Factor, a measure of how well sunscreen will protect skin from the sun's damaging rays

whisk
a quick movement, but also the name for a kitchen tool used to beat ingredients together

Books to read

Future Fuels to Fight Climate Change by Rachel Kehoe (Focus Readers, 2023)
This book will tell you about the harm caused by using fossil fuels for energy, plus the sources of energy that humans can use instead: solar, water, wind, and other renewable forms of energy.

Get Into Science: Full of Energy by Jane Lacey (Franklin Watts, 2020)
Basic information about energy (from plant to animal and energy from the sun) is explained with fun illustrations, as well as challenges and activities to try.

Quick Fix Science: Light and *Quick Fix Science: Forces and Magnetism* by Paul Mason (Wayland, 2021)
Meet Snappy, a young Nile crocodile. Snappy is really interested in science, but not all that good at it yet! In these books, Snappy finds out more about light (which is a form of energy), and forces (which are the physical effects of energy).

Brownie ingredients

If you want to make the same brownies as Mo and Rory, here are the ingredients:

- 1 cup (2 sticks) unsalted butter
- 8 ounces semisweet chocolate chips
- 1/2 cup all-purpose flour
- 1/2 cup cocoa powder
- 1 cup granulated sugar
- 1 cup dark brown sugar
- 4 large eggs
- 1/2 teaspoon salt
- 2 teaspoons vanilla extract

You can find the whole recipe they followed at:
www.foodnetwork.com/recipes/fudgey-brownies-3623230

Make sure you read the safety instructions at the beginning of the book!

Answers

Page 7

They all need the sun, for food, warmth, or both.

Page 17

Ice melts when heat energy is added to it.

Wax in candles also changes from solid to liquid because of heat energy.

Metal changes to a liquid as well, but metal needs a lot more heat energy than ice or candles do.

In fact, everything solid can become liquid if enough heat energy is added. Some materials need a LOT of heat energy, though. Diamonds, for example, only melt when heated to 6,322°F (3,550°C)!

Page 27

1) is c): a circuit.

2) is d): all of those. a) and c) would mean there was no circuit for the electricity to flow around; b) would mean there was no electricity.